ANIMALS

SILLY SCIENCE FOR SMART KIDS

Written by

Robin Twiddy

Designed & illustrated by

Amy Li

BookLife
PUBLISHING

©2020
BookLife Publishing Ltd.
King's Lynn
Norfolk, PE30 4LS

ISBN: 978-1-78637-996-2

Written by:
Robin Twiddy

Edited by:
Madeline Tyler

Designed by:
Amy Li

PHOTO CREDITS: Images are courtesy of Shutterstock.com.
With thanks to Getty Images, Thinkstock Photo and iStockPhoto.
Cover: bosotochka, sumstock, hellofakeworld, Recurring Images: bosotochka (header font), Sonechko57 (blobs), Amy Li (additional illustrations). P2–3 – Dima Zel, p4–5 – ONYXprj, Ovocheva, Andrey Korshenkov, kuban_girl, Akifune, zhu difeng, Chinch, p6–7 – Eric Isslee, Vectorpocket, Panda Vector, New Africa, SofiaV, p8–9 – Krenegade (wiki commons), Beverly Speed, M.Stasy, BigMouse, SilvieMiskova, lukpedclub, Richard Whitcombe, Zimniy, Baskiabat, p10–11 – andregric, Kastoluza, Nadya_Art, Olesia, Bilkei, peart, fizkes, p12–13 – A7880S, Alla Pogrebnaya, J HIME, Olga Kononok, derter, p14–15 – fivespots, Ekaterina Kapranova, DestinoSalvaje, CoSveta, KingVector, wavebreakmedia, p16–17 – AlexanderTrou, Alfmaler, GoodStudio, Iconic Bestiary, MicroOne, ONYXprj, Pixel-Shot, Ramy Fathalla, vectortatu, p18–19 – Andrea Izzotti, fatamorgana-999, Jung Hsuan, RaiDztor, robuart, Baskiabat, p20–21 – Danita Delmont, xpixel, VitaliyVill, Spreadthesign, Maquiladora, p22–23 – fokusgood, andras_csontos, andriano.cz, Nerthuz, Baskiabat, Visual Generation, sunflowerr, p24–25 – Aaron Amat, Astrovector, bogdanhoda, Dmitry Kalinovsky, Nico Faramaz, Viktoriya Belova, p26–27 – Pixelheld, StockSmartStart, Isarapic, Aleksandar Dickov, MarcoVector, Sudowoodo, Martin Pelanek, Yukihipo, p28–29 – Maquiladora, Everett Historical, IMissisHope, NotionPic, Vectors Bang, Zaie, Baskiabat

CONTENTS

Words that look like **THIS** are explained in the glossary on page 31.

SCIENCE:
Why So Serious?

We all know science, don't we? Boring people in boring white coats, writing boring things on boring clipboards. Boring, boring, boring, right? Wrong! What if I told you that science can be sillier than you have ever imagined?

SILLY
Animals

All work and no play makes Fluffy a dull boy!

Animals can be very serious. They go to the bank, iron underpants and never have too much chocolate. Wait, that's not right. That sounds like boring adults. Very boring *human* adults. Animals are much sillier, and so is the science that surrounds them.

Welcome to the

SILLY ZONE

You are about to enter the Silly Zone. In this book you will find scientists doing the strangest things. Get ready!

Real

SCIENCE

Even though science can sometimes seem very silly, there is always a very good reason for it. In the 1700s, a scientist dressed frogs up in tiny trousers to see if this stopped them from making baby frogs. It did! This also helped the scientific community understand **REPRODUCTION** better.

KOALA Crimes

Come out with your Paws in the Air - You're Under ARREST!

So, no koalas were actually arrested, but one did nearly ruin a police investigation. How? By touching things. Police in Australia found that koalas and human beings have really, really, really similar fingerprints. But why is that a problem?

Fingerprints are completely UNIQUE. No two people have the same fingerprints, and neither do koalas.

One way that police gather **EVIDENCE** at a crime scene is to dust for fingerprints. To do this, they spread a fine powder over areas they think have been touched. The powder sticks to the natural oils left by fingers. Using a soft brush, the detective will remove the extra powder.

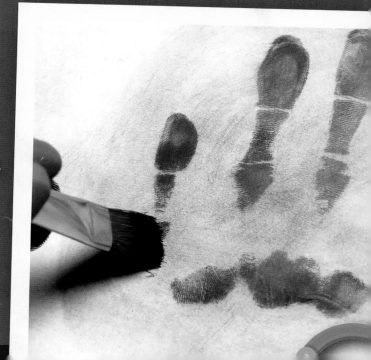

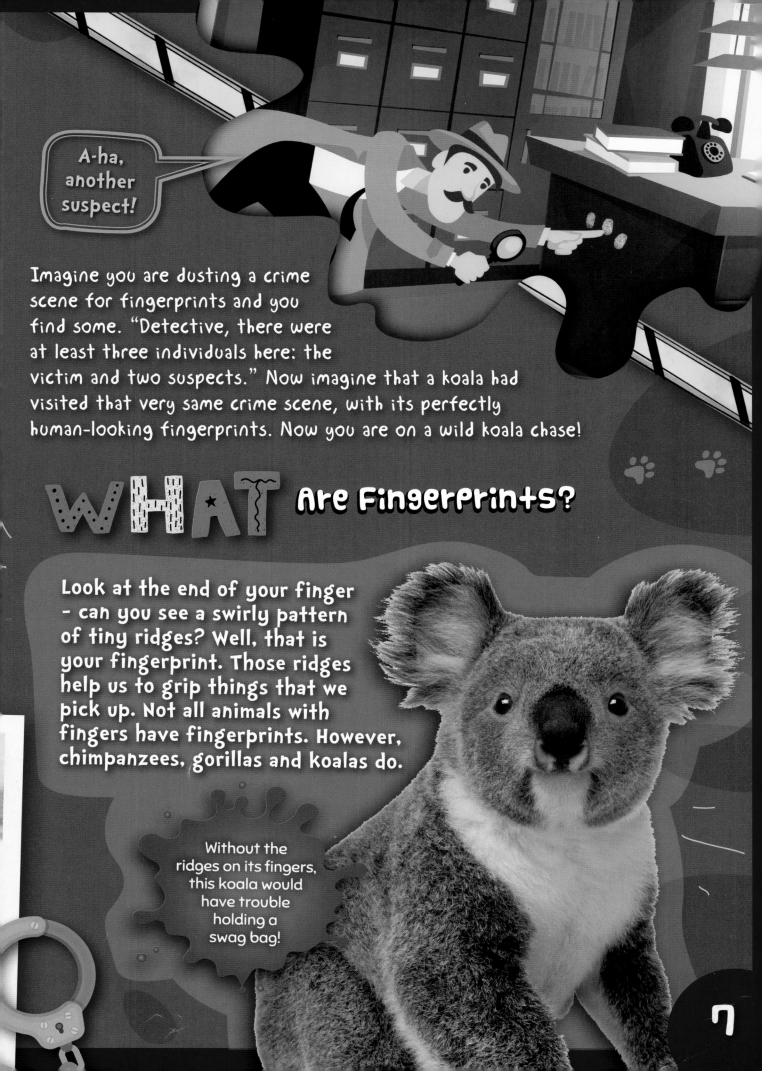

A-ha, another suspect!

Imagine you are dusting a crime scene for fingerprints and you find some. "Detective, there were at least three individuals here: the victim and two suspects." Now imagine that a koala had visited that very same crime scene, with its perfectly human-looking fingerprints. Now you are on a wild koala chase!

WHAT Are Fingerprints?

Look at the end of your finger - can you see a swirly pattern of tiny ridges? Well, that is your fingerprint. Those ridges help us to grip things that we pick up. Not all animals with fingers have fingerprints. However, chimpanzees, gorillas and koalas do.

Without the ridges on its fingers, this koala would have trouble holding a swag bag!

Fist of the MANTIS
(Shrimp)

Mantis STYLE

The greatest martial artists train their entire lives to punch the hardest and fastest, and to be the best they can be. The fastest punch ever recorded was thrown by Keith Liddell, a boxer from Chicago in the US. His punch was recorded at over 72 kilometres per hour. That's fast!

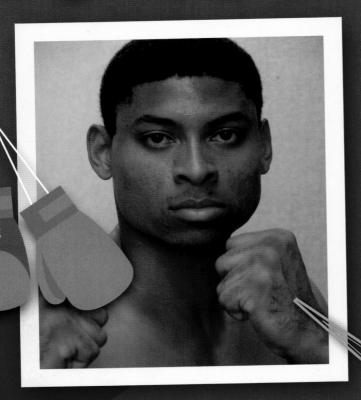

> I have lightning-fast fists!

Fastest PUNCH in the World

Even though the record for the fastest punch in the world is held by a human, the record should really go to a creature that is only ten centimetres long – the mantis shrimp.

> Who are you calling small? Come down here and say that!

TOO QUICK
to Capture

Scientists knew that this little shrimp punched fast enough to break glass, but what they did not know was that the shrimp punched faster than their cameras could capture. The scientists had to use high-speed cameras to study it.

POWER Punch

The high-speed cameras showed something very interesting. When the mantis punched, there was a small flash of light. This is caused by a change in **PRESSURE** in the water, which causes it to boil. When the water boils, small bubbles are formed that collapse when the pressure returns to normal. This releases a huge amount of energy, adding to the power of the punch.

Kamehameka...

This kind of energy release is called cavitation.

RODENT

ROFL TICKLE Time

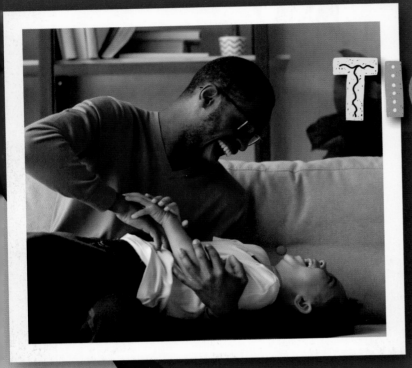

A hand reaches from above. Fingers wriggle as they get closer to your body. When they finally touch you, you begin to laugh uncontrollably. What are you? The surprising answer is a rat in a cage.

I Tickle RATS

A team of scientists tickle rats and get paid for it. But why are they doing something so silly? What on earth can we learn from tickling rats?

HA-HA

Stop, stop. That tickles!

Ultrasonic
SQUEALS

Rats laugh when you tickle them. You can't hear it because it is in a higher **FREQUENCY** than humans can hear, but they are doing it. This silly science has actually taught us a lot.

Don't be a silly billy. You can't hear that rat laugh without special equipment.

I'm having a bad day – can someone tickle me?

What Rat-Tickling
TAUGHT US

Rats won't laugh when tickled if they aren't happy - just like people. The same area in rat and human brains is activated when tickled. Rats who were tickled were observed making better decisions and generally being happier.

Some scientists believe that this will help us understand why humans are ticklish.

The Wandering WONDER Dog

NO Trains, Planes or Automobiles

He travelled 4,105 kilometres (km) to get home. He travelled by foot, without a compass or a map, and without being able to ask for directions. He is Bobbie the Wandering Wonder Dog!

Bobbie's family lost him while they were on holiday together. They looked everywhere for him but eventually had to head home without him.

The TREK

When Bobbie finally made it home to his family after six months, he was mangy, dirty and showed clear signs that he had walked the entire journey, including crossing rivers and mountain ranges in winter. How did he do it? How did he find his way home?

Wait, that is not home. That is a tortoise.

SMELL
You Later

Scientists believe that dogs use familiar scents to find their way home. They know that dogs can follow a scent for up to 16 km. But Bobbie couldn't smell his family from 4,105 km away.

Pit STOPS

Bobbie's family regularly stopped at **REST STOPS** on their journey across the country. People told newspapers that Bobbie had stopped at these same stops on his return journey. Perhaps Bobbie followed the scent from one stop to the next until he finally made it home.

Welcome home, Bobbie.

Miracle LIZARD

What IS SO SPECIAL?

Can you walk on water? You can't? Well, don't feel bad about it — most people can't. But the basilisk lizard can. It is not easy to do. You need more than belief to walk on water. You need special feet.

Walking on water is not as easy as it sounds!

SECRET
Weapon Number One

So, how does the basilisk lizard manage to stay on top of the water? Its first secret weapon is its special feet. The basilisk lizard has extra scales between its toes on its hind legs.

Special feet for a special lizard

The SECOND Secret Weapon

The basilisk's second secret weapon is how fast it slams those special feet onto the water. The feet hit the water so quickly that they trap a pocket of air between the lizard and the water.

Run, lizard, run!

SUPER Lizard

So, really, more impressive than walking on water, the basilisk lizard is actually running on air! Scientists believe that we might be able to make machines that can travel across water thanks to what we know about the basilisk lizard.

Move over, Superman. Make room for the basilisk lizard.

Why You Never See PIGEONS at the Cinema

Oops...

"Amazing. 5 crumbs out of 5!" - The Daily Coo

SAVING PRIVATE PIGEON

PRODUCTION
SCENE CUT TAKE
DATE ROLL
PROD
DIRECTOR CAMERA

IS It the PRICE?

Have you ever been watching a film at the cinema and thought to yourself, "Where are all the pigeons? I bet they would love this film." You would be wrong! It is a scientific fact that pigeons don't like any films.

For my next trick, I will bring pictures to life.

It's an ILLUSION

So, why don't pigeons like films? It has to do with the **ILLUSION** that makes thousands of still images appear as though they are one moving image. Films show 24 still images, called frames, every second. This makes it look like the pictures are moving.

EYE of the Pigeon

I can see you moving.

24 frames per second is fast enough to fool the human eye, but pigeons have **EVOLVED** a good sense for detecting movement. This helps them to see live **PREY** from a distance and to spot predators sneaking up on them.

A Series of PICTURES

If a pigeon was watching a film at the cinema, it would just see a series of still images. To make a film that pigeons would enjoy, it would need to be shown at 75 frames per second.

At 24 frames per second, it would be as if the humans were showing the pigeons a slideshow of their best holiday pictures.

... and then we went to this bridge. Marge said it was the best bridge she had ever seen.

This is so boring!

I pooped on that bridge.

17

Pom Pom POW

DEADLY Cheerleaders

This tiny little crab, about the size of a penny, may look like it is cheering on its favourite sports team, but those are no normal pom poms.

A Fist FULL of Anemones

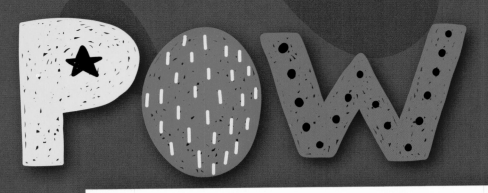

Pom Pom crab

Hey, Nippy, you're so fine. You're so fine you blow my mind, hey Nippy!

Those are sea anemones it is holding. Sea anemones are creatures that live in the ocean. Anemones can't move around on their own, but they do have lots of stinging tentacles.

Sea anemone

Anemones for My
ENEMIES

These crabs use those anemones to pack extra pow into their punches. This is why they are also known as boxer crabs. The anemone-punch can help them to see off predators and to catch lunch.

I could have been a contender, Charlie.

TW for One

Unlike other crabs that have big strong claws for nipping and crushing, the pom pom crab has thin, tweezer-like claws that it uses to hold the anemones. If it loses one, the crab can tear its remaining anemone in two!

Hey, you look familiar.

The anemones torn in half regrow as perfect **CLONES** of the original anemone!

We are clones. I am practically you!

BLOOD

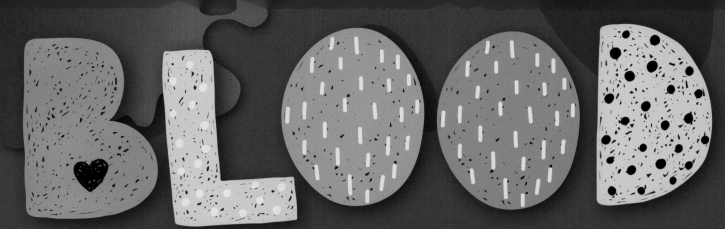

IS in the Eye of the Beholder

Don't CRY for Me, Horned Lizard (Because It's Gross)

In the North American deserts, there roams a lizard with an unusual way of protecting itself. It cries blood.

Hey, I don't cry. I squirt it out of my eyes.

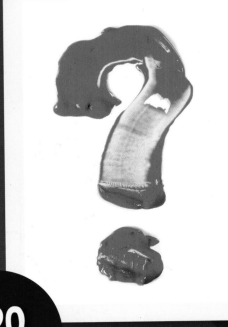

WHY Squirt Blood?

Because it is fun? No. Is it a sport? No. It actually uses it to stop predators. Squirting blood out of its eyes isn't just scary — the lizard squirts it straight into the mouths of hungry predators.

YOU TASTE Terrible

So why is this a good idea? Surely giving predators a taste of you in advance is a pretty silly idea. Maybe science can give us an answer to this.

TRY Before You Buy

Those silly scientists! They actually tested the blood from the horned lizards' eyes and found that it contained a chemical that is really unpleasant to taste. Dogs really dislike it.

FREE TASTE TEST
9/10 predators prefer the taste of other lizards.

SLIME
Trousers?

EWW

Sometimes, science isn't just silly, it is downright disgusting. How would you feel if you found out that your trousers were made of **MUCUS**? Sticky, I imagine.

HAGFISH

The hagfish, sometimes also known as the slime eel, is a creature found in oceans all around the world. It gets its name from its defence mechanism. When it is attacked, it produces huge amounts of slime very quickly.

Well, I went in for the kill and suddenly there was all this slime every-where. It was awful. I couldn't breathe. It's just not right, you know!

SLIMY
Science

When scientists started looking closely at the slime from the hagfish, they noticed something interesting. There were long **FIBRES** in the slime, almost like really strong lengths of cotton.

Yuck! I have just had a disgusting idea!

The MATERIAL of the Future

These very clever yet very silly scientists believe that they can make clothes from these fibres, or possibly **ARTIFICIALLY** recreate the hagfish slime fibres in a lab.

SALE

Slime clothes
90% off
All slime must go!

Lyre, Lyre, BEAKS on Fire

What IS That I HEAR?

Imagine you are in the woods. It is peaceful and quiet. Then you hear a chainsaw. You run to where the sound is coming from but there are no people there. You look down to find a brown bird.

MIMICRY

This is the lyrebird, nature's greatest **MIMIC**. The lyrebird can make almost any sound it has heard before. Mostly, the lyrebird mimics other birds found in the forest and uses the sounds in his **MATING DANCE**.

SING
While You Work

As people get closer to the homes of the lyrebird, the birds are hearing more and more human sounds. One lyrebird at a zoo tormented staff with a perfect copy of construction sounds, such as drills and hammers, for weeks after the construction crew had left.

Watch me confuse these birds. Hahahahaha.

Scientific
SILLINESS

Scientists recorded a lyrebird mimicking a grey shrike-thrush (a small Australian bird). Almost every time they played the lyrebird's recording, a grey shrike-thrush would approach looking for a mate.

The MYSTERY
of the Cubic POO

We did it!

Let's Talk About POO

Imagine — there are hundreds of scientists all gathered together. On the stage is one very excited scientist. "We did it," he shouts. "We did it. We know how the wombat poos cubes!"

The GREAT Mystery

For years, people have wondered how wombats do it. No other animal in the world can poo out a perfect cube. Only the wombat can do that and, until recently, nobody knew how.

Who wants to see a party trick?

Poo normally comes in one of three forms:
- **CYLINDRICAL**
- Pellet-shaped
- Watery

SQUARE
Poo in a Round Hole

How does a **CUBIC** poo come from a round hole? To answer this question, scientists inflated balloons inside a wombat's digestive system. From this, they learnt that it was in the final part of the **INTESTINE** that the poo takes on its unique shape.

Well, Mr Wombat. I have a party trick involving this balloon, but I don't think you are going to like it!

How do they make them that shape?

Silly Science in ACTION

It is believed that studying how wombats make cubic poos could teach us a new way to manufacture cube-shaped objects. That means that in the future, there might be machines in factories based on the wombat's intestine.

The Great OCTODINI

WHO -Dini?

Harry Houdini is probably the most famous **ESCAPE ARTIST** of all time. He was famous for death-defying escapes on stage that shocked and baffled his audiences. But there is one animal who beats Houdini every time.

Harry Houdini stepping into a crate to be lowered into New York Harbour

INKY the ESCAPING OCTOPUS

Inky the octopus lived at the New Zealand Aquarium until one day when he decided to head back to the ocean. Staff came in the next morning to find his aquarium empty.

Where's the octopus?

Smart and SQUIDGY

Because octopuses do not have any bones, they can squeeze through very small spaces. Inky did just that. Workers at the aquarium believe that Inky squeezed through a small gap in the top of his tank, crawled across the floor and escaped down a drainpipe to the sea.

Octopuses are very CURIOUS and like to explore.

THE SEA

I've got half of my legs in... I can taste the freedom!

GENIUS of the sea

Scientists have carried out many tests that prove how smart octopuses are. They can solve puzzles and use shells and coconuts to hide in. Without being super smart, Inky never would have made it out of the aquarium.

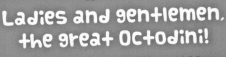

Ladies and gentlemen, the great Octodini!

ANIMALS

Do the Silliest Things !

Animal

SCIENCE

Animals can be silly, but so can scientists. If you put them both together, you get something very silly. Tickling rats and clothes made from fish slime... What are these scientists thinking?!

SILLY + Silly = ...

The silliest thing is how many useful things can be learnt from silly scientists playing silly games with silly animals. It would seem that sometimes, silly + silly = serious science!

GLOSSARY

artificially — made or done by humans in a way that is not natural

clones — copies of something or someone that are exactly the same

cubic — in the shape of a cube — you know, boxy like a box

curious — keen to explore and learn more

cylindrical — in the shape of a cylinder — you know, tubey like a loo roll

escape artist — a performer who specialises in escaping from impossible situations

evidence — something that gives proof and can be used to give reason to believe something

evolved — gradually developed and adapted to an environment over a long time

fibres — things that are like threads

frequency — the measurement of sound waves

illusion — something that appears to be real or true but is not

intestine — the lower part of the digestive tract leading from the stomach to the anus (bottom)

mating dance — a way that some animals attract mates through dance and song

mimic — a thing that copies other things

mucus — the thick, slippery liquid produced by many linings in the body, such as the inside of the nose

pressure — a continuous physical force that acts on an object, which is caused by something pressing against it

prey — animals that are hunted by other animals for food

reproduction — making more of the same type of thing

rest stops — areas along roads for people to stop and rest, often including places to eat and sleep

unique — special or unusual; unlike anything else

INDEX